Wine Time
A Coloring Book for Adults

illustrated by
Rachel Jones

FREE BONUS PAGES

Visit http://racheljonesarts.com/wine-time/ to receive a PDF of 5 Bonus Coloring Pages.

Just have
a glass of
wine

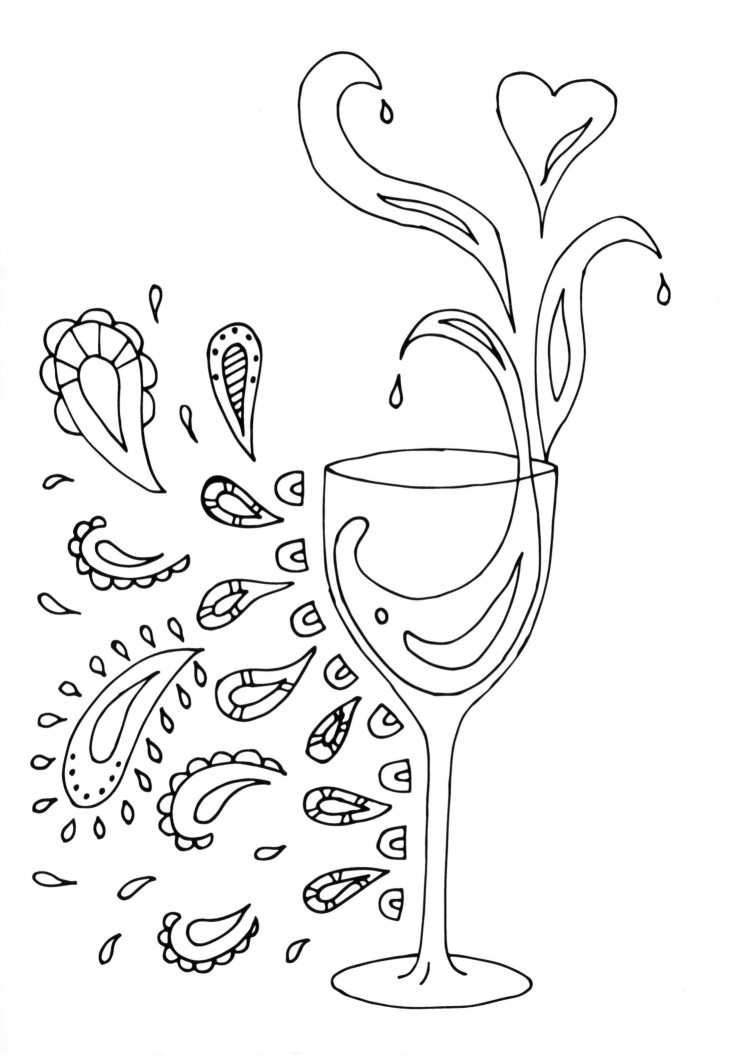

Smile, There's Wine

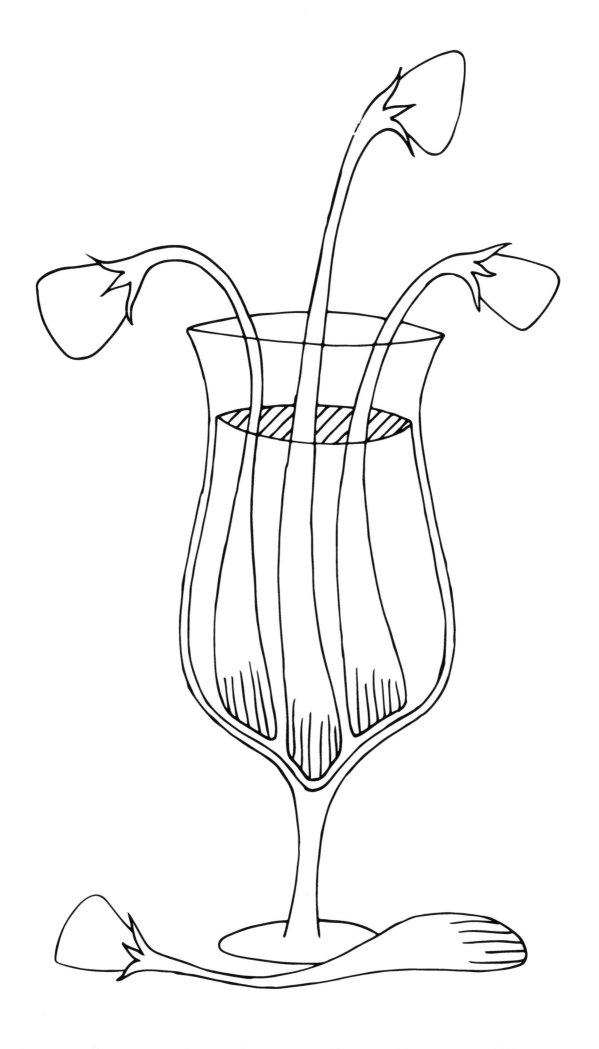

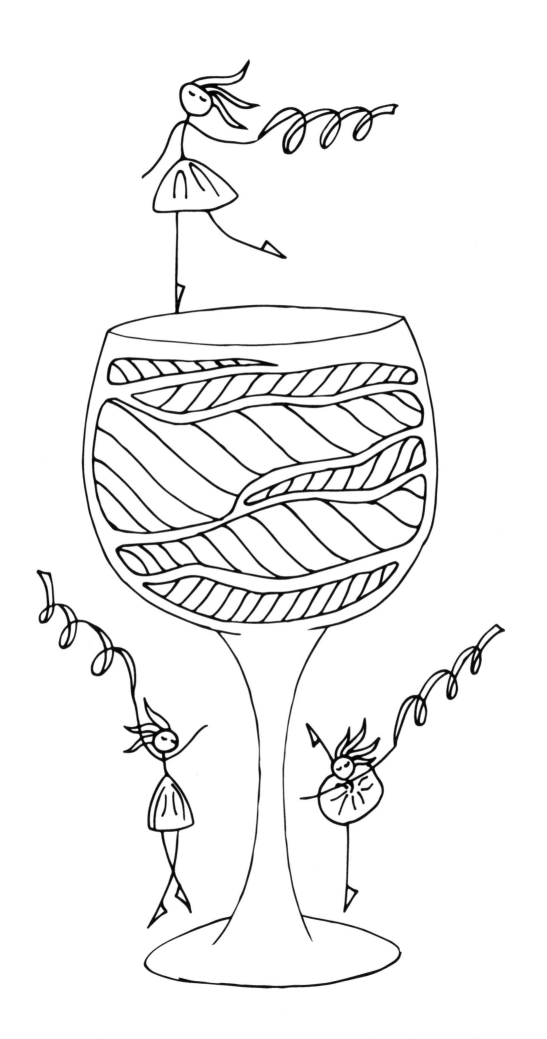

Made in the USA
Middletown, DE
10 December 2016